THE FOUNDATION

This book is approved by Zac Brown Band

Arranged by Jeff Jacobson

Cherry Lane Music Company
Director of Publications/Project Editor: Mark Phillips

ISBN 978-1-60378-310-1

Visit our website at www.cherrylaneprint.com

THE FOUNDATION

On November 18, 2008, Atlantic Records/Home Grown/Big Picture released Zac Brown Band's *The Foundation*, a collection of 12 songs that drew inspiration from the band's Southern roots and everyday life experiences. It's music that resonates no matter where you call home.

Zac Brown Band's signature sound is equal parts country, bluegrass, Southern rock, pop, and reggae. Led by the tenacious Zac Brown, the band possesses awe-inspiring musicianship, skillful songwriting, and dynamic live performances that have been embraced by audiences across the country. "Chicken Fried," the album's first single, sold almost 150,000 downloads in its first five weeks of release, and established the band as a radio favorite.

Produced by the legendary Keith Stegall (Alan Jackson, George Jones), *The Foundation* features "Whatever It Is," a ballad about the bewildering power of love; "Toes," an ode to the pleasures of beach life; and "Free," which has turned into an audience anthem during tour stops.

Zac Brown Band performs upwards of 250 dates a year and has played more than 3,000 shows in their career, sharing the stage with such artists as Sugarland, Alan Jackson, Los Lonely Boys, the Allman Brothers, Willie Nelson, B.B. King, ZZ Top, and Etta James. The band's aggressive touring has helped them develop a fanatical grassroots following by winning over believers one person at a time. "There's no way to predict how fast everything is going to come together," says Zac, "or that it took 13 years to get to the beginning of it."

"Zac Brown Band is a self-made American success story," says Atlantic Records Chairman/CEO Craig Kallman. "They've built up a phenomenal grassroots base with music that cuts across musical boundaries and walks of life to speak to the hearts of people everywhere. They are the perfect band for our times, with the songs, the musicianship, and the power to become a major presence."

Zac Brown Band is: singer/guitarist Zac Brown, fiddler Jimmy De Martini, bassist John Hopkins, guitarist/organist Coy Bowles, and drummer Chris Fryar.

PRAISE FOR ZAC BROWN BAND'S *THE FOUNDATION*:

"The Zac Brown Band creates the kind of idiosyncratic pastiche that homogenously efficient Nashville can neither produce nor predict. Still, it's music made for singing along, for dancing along, and for drinking along. In a genre in desperate need of fresh blood, Brown's a welcome infusion."—*USA Today*

"Zac Brown Band's major-label debut is as refreshing a set as has come down the pike in quite some time."—*Billboard*

"Full of soul and freewheeling tales..."—*Billboard*

"Brown and his band have cooked up a delicious sound made up of different ingredients with an undeniable Southern streak running through it all."—*Memphis Commercial Appeal*

"Brown and his band have the potential to broaden the definition of country music, a worthy accomplishment."—*Orlando Sentinel*

"*The Foundation* blends traditional country with jam band–style Southern rock, bluegrass, and even a touch of reggae."—*Atlanta Journal Constitution*

CONTENTS

TOES

Words and Music by
Zac Brown, Wyatt Durrette,
John Driskell Hopkins and Shawn Mullins

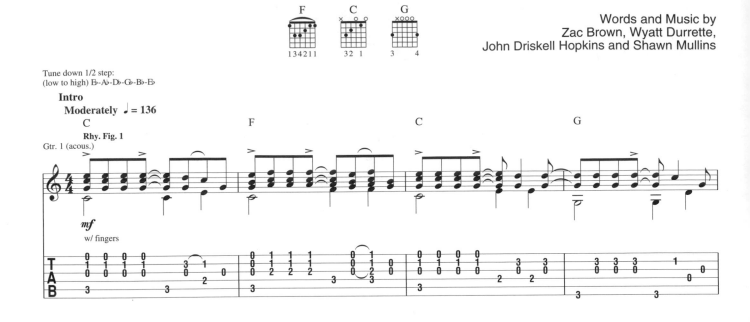

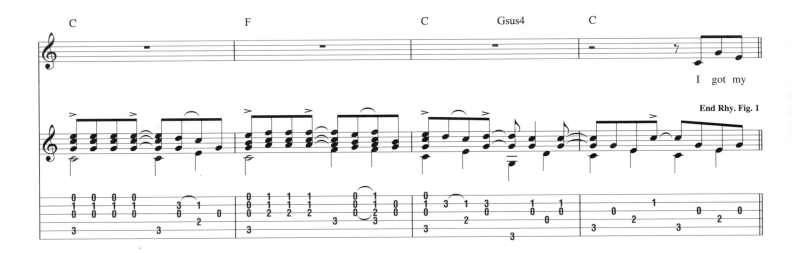

Gtr. 1: w/ Rhy. Fill 1

C   N.C.

I'd have no rea - son ___ to stay. _____
when I throw pe - sos ___ their way. _____   Ad - i - os and va - ya ___ con
and I got no mon - ey ___ to stay. _____

To Coda 2

F   C
Gtr. 1

Di - os.   Yeah, I'm leav - ing G - A. _____
                  A long way ___ from G - A. _____
                  Go - ing home ___ now to stay. ___

To Coda 1

G

(2nd time, cont in notation)

Gon - na lay in the hot sun and roll a big fat one and, and grab my gui - tar ___ and
Some - one do me a fa - vor and pour me some Jae - ger and I'll grab my gui - tar ___ and

Gtr. 1: w/ Rhy. Fig. 1
C   F   C   G

play.

C   F   C   Gsus4   C

2. Well, four days ___

Verse
Gtr. 1: w/ Rhy. Fig. 3
C   F   C   G

___ flew by ___ like a drunk Fri - day night ___ as the sum - mer drew ___ to an end. ___ They ___

C   F   C   G   C

___ can't be - lieve ___ that I just ___ could - n't leave, ___ and I bid ___ a - dieu ___ to my friends. ___ 'Cause my ___

7

___ bar - tend - er, ___ she's ___ from the is - lands; her bod - y's been kissed ___ by the sun. ___ And

D.S. al Coda 1

co-co-nut re - plac-es the smell ___ of the bar, ___ and I don't ___ know if it's her ___ or the rum. ___ I got my

let ring - - - - - - - - - - - - - - - - - -

Coda 1

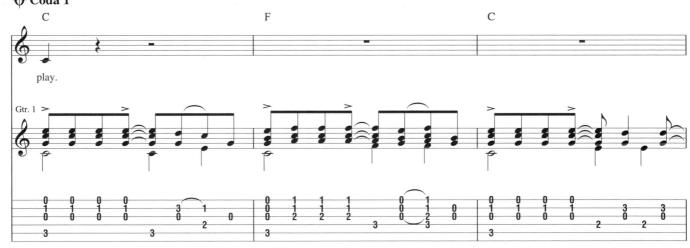

play.

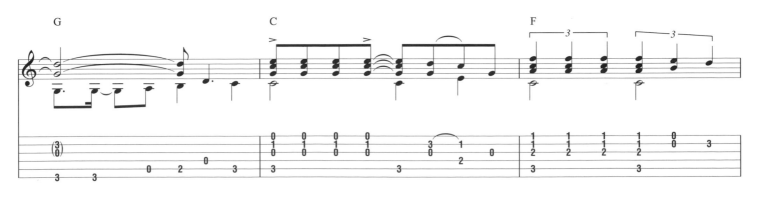

WHATEVER IT IS

Words and Music by
Zac Brown and Wyatt Durrette

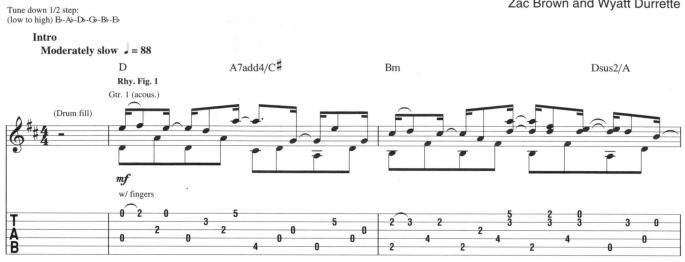

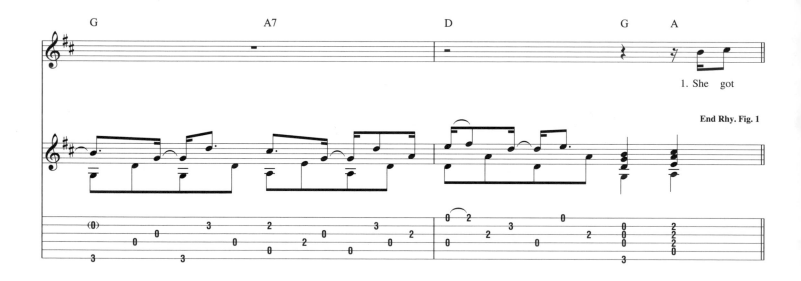

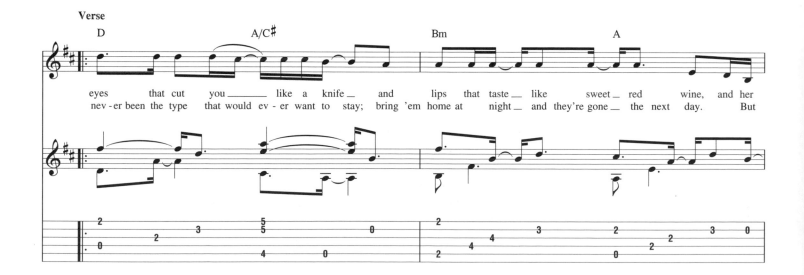

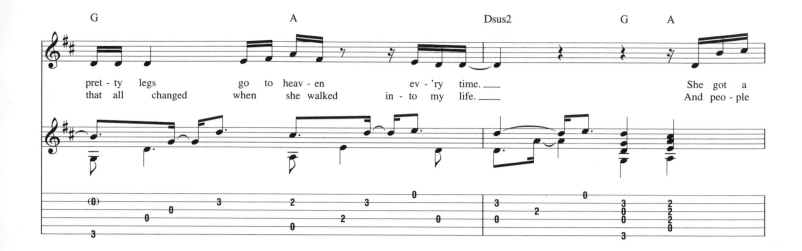

pret - ty legs __ go to heav - en ev - 'ry time. __ She got a
that all changed when she walked in - to my life. __ And peo - ple

gen - tle way __ that puts me at ease; __ when she walks in the room I can hard - ly breathe. __ Got a
ask - in' why it is, tell 'em I don't know, there's just some - thin' 'bout the wom - an makes my heart go __ hay - wire.

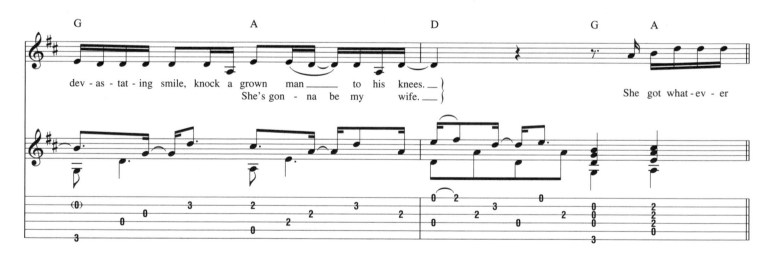

dev - as - tat - ing smile, knock a grown man __ to his knees. }
She's gon - na be my wife. __ }   She got what - ev - er

𝄋 Chorus

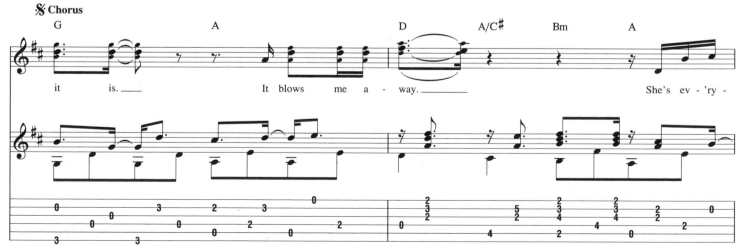

it is. __   It blows me a - way. __   She's ev - 'ry -

11

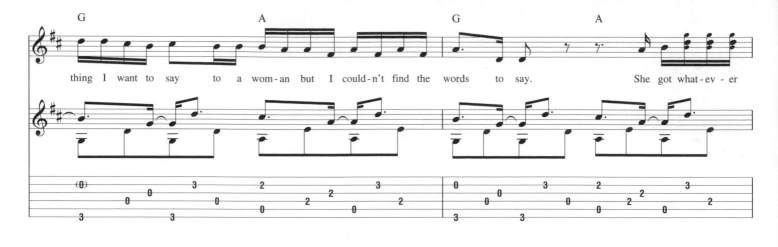

thing I want to say   to a wom-an but I could-n't find the words   to say.   She got what-ev - er

it is. ___   I don't know what to do. ___   'Cause ev - 'ry

To Coda ⊕

time I try to tell her how I feel, _ it comes _ out _ "I ___ love you." _   You got what-ev - er

Pitch: A   D   G

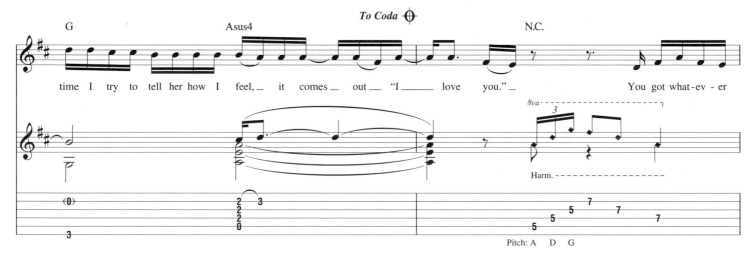

Gtr. 1: w/ Rhy. Fig. 1

|1.

|2.

it is.   2. You know, I've

Gtr. 1

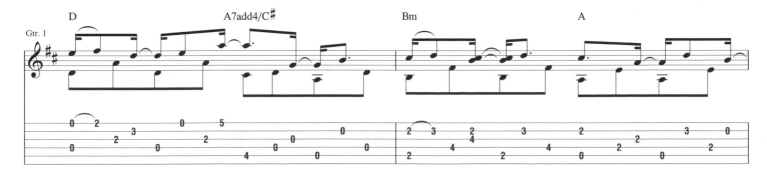

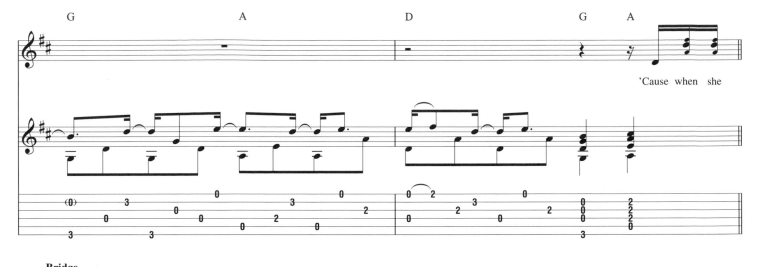

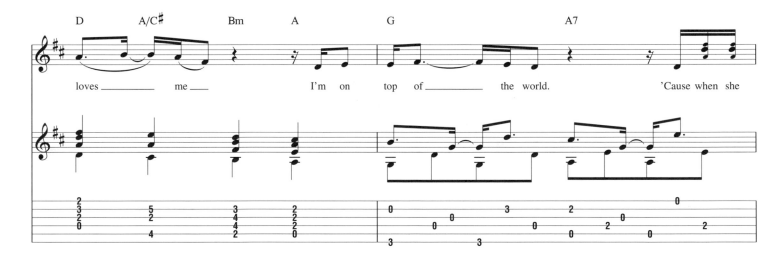

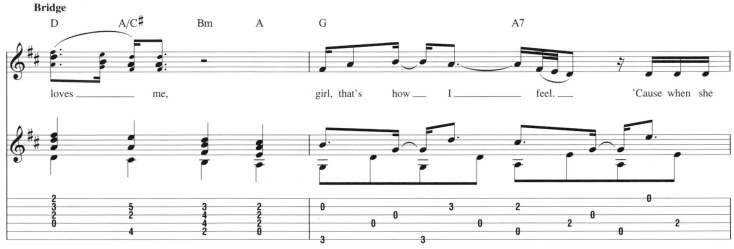

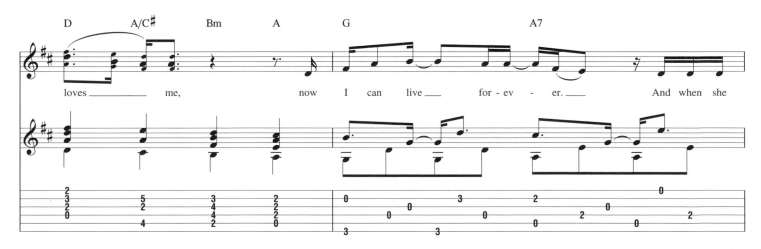

loves ___ me ___ I am un-touch-a-ble.___ She got what-ev-er

Coda

Outro

___ love you." ___ I do. You got what-ev-er it is.

Oh, _____ you got what-ev-er it is.

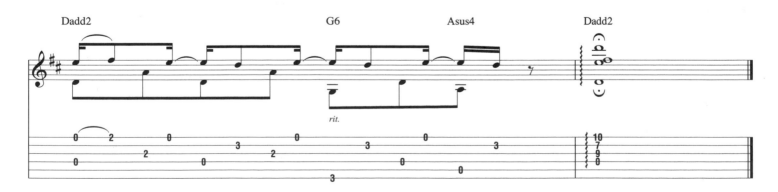

rit.

WHERE THE BOAT LEAVES FROM

Words and Music by
Zac Brown and Wyatt Durrette

trop - i - cal__ lips that are sing - ing:_____ Get a -

Chorus

way__ to where the boat leaves from;__ it takes a - way__ all of your

big prob - lems.__ You got wor - ries, you can drop 'em in the blue o - cean.__ But you

got - ta get a - way to where the boat leaves from. So get a - way__ to where the

boat leaves from;__ it takes a - way__ all of your big prob - lems.__ You got

wor - ries, you can drop 'em in the blue o - cean.__ But you got - ta get a - way to where the...

So get a - way__ to where the boat leaves from;__ it takes a -

way__ all of your big prob - lems.__ You got wor - ries, you can drop 'em in the

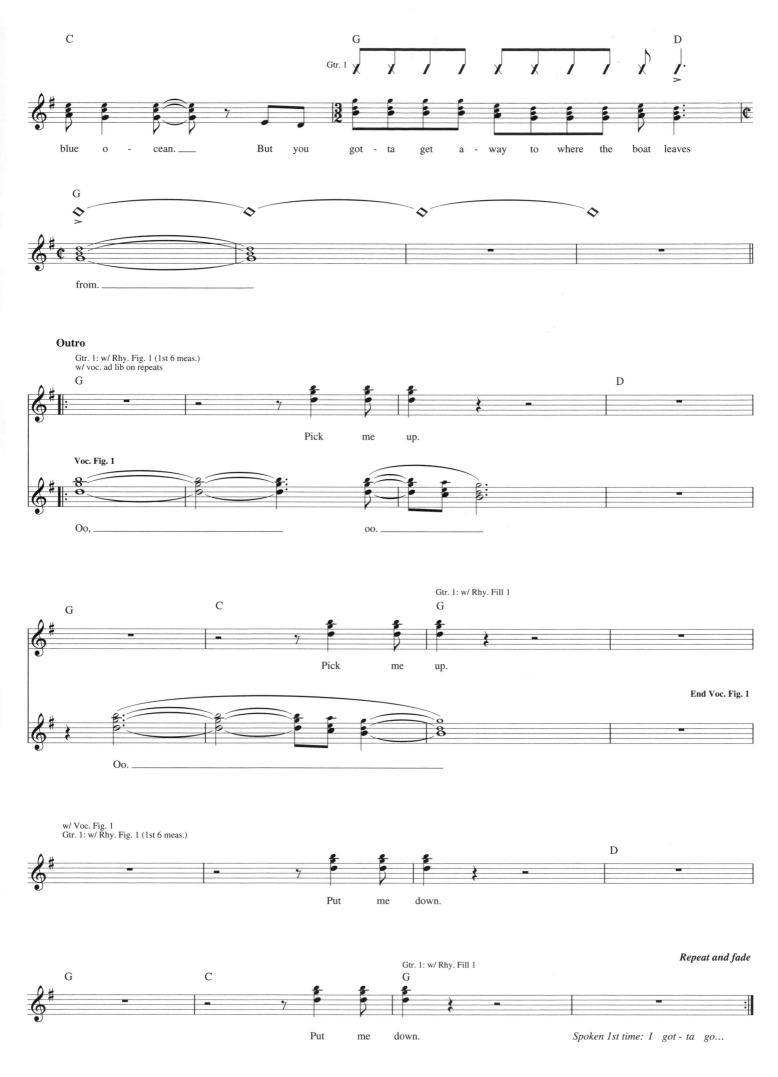

Outro

FREE

Words and Music by
Zac Brown

*Drop D tuning, down 1/2 step, partial capo II:
(low to high) Db-Ab-Db-Gb-Bb-Eb

Intro

Moderately slow, in 2 ♩ = 76

C

Rhy. Fig. 1

Gtr. 1 (acous.)

mp

w/ fingers

*6th string is not capoed. Using a clip-on style capo, place from underneath neck onto highest five strings only. Alternatively, use drop C tuning (without capo) up 1/2 step:
(low to high) C#-A#-D#-G#-B#-E#, and play tab as written.

**All music is indicated relative to capo key (key of C). Capoed fret (strings 1-5) is "0" in tab.

Fmaj7

1. So

End Rhy. Fig. 1

Verse

Gtr. 1: w/ Rhy. Fig. 1 (1 1/2 times)

C

we live out in our ___ old van, ___ trav-el all a-cross ___ this land, ___
drive un-til the cit - y lights ___ dis-solve in-to a coun-try sky, ___ just

Fmaj7

me and ___ you. ___
me and ___ you. ___

C

We'll end up hand ___ in hand ___ some-where down ___ on the sand, ___ just
Lay un-der-neath the har - vest moon, ___ do all the things that lov-ers do, ___ just

strum w/ fingers

Bridge

No, we don't ___ have a lot of mon - ey. No, we don't ___

*Gtr. 1: w/ Rhy. Fig. 1 (last 4 meas.)

Fmaj7

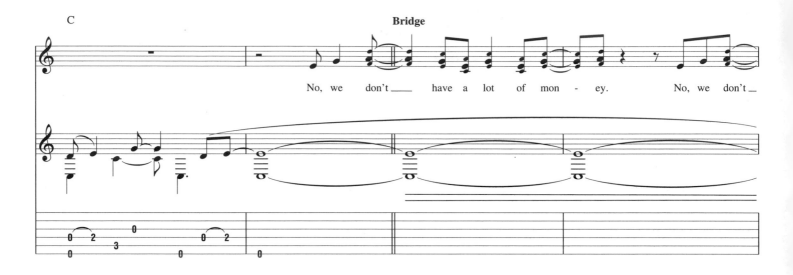

___ have a lot of mon - ey. No, we don't ___ have a lot of mon - ey. No, we don't ___

*; grad. cresc. next 12 meas.

Gtr. 1: w/ Rhy. Fig. 1

C

___ have a lot of mon - ey. No, we don't ___ have a lot of mon - ey. No, we don't ___

Fmaj7

___ have a lot of mon - ey. No, we don't ___ have a lot of mon - ey.

CHICKEN FRIED

Words and Music by
Zac Brown and Wyatt Durrette

Verse
Half-time feel
Gtr. 1: w/ Rhy. Fig. 2

fun-ny how ___ it's the lit-tle things ___ in life ___ that mean the most; not

End half-time feel

where you live, ___ what you drive, ___ or the price tag on your clothes. ___ There's no

Gtr. 1

dol-lar sign ___ on peace of mind; ___ this I've come to know. So if

D.S. al Coda 1

you a-gree, ___ have a drink with me; ___ raise your glass-es for a toast ___ to a lit-tle bit of

⊕ Coda 1

Violin Solo
Gtr. 1: w/ Rhy. Fig. 3 (last meas.)   Gtr. 1: w/ Rhy. Fig. 3 (2 times)

(Sing 1st time only)

Gtr. 1

w/ fingers

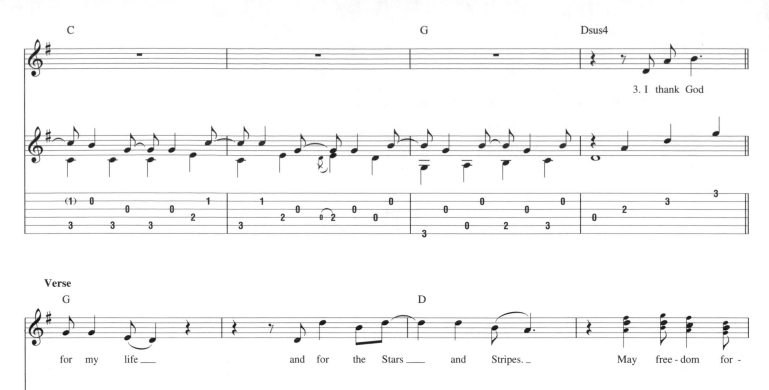

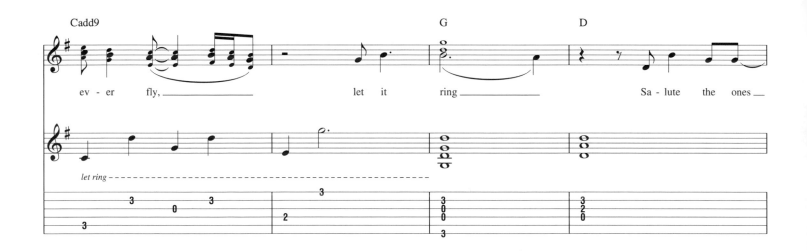

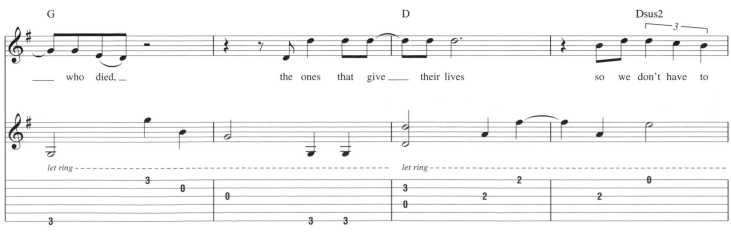

MARY

Words and Music by
Zac Brown and Jay Cline

*Tune down 1/2 step, capo V:
(low to high) E♭-A♭-D♭-G♭-B♭-E♭

Intro

Moderately fast, in 2 ♩ = 148

*Equivalent to standard tuning, capo IV.

**All music sounds a major third higher than indicated due to capo and tuning. Capoed fret is "0" in tab.

Chorus

Mar - y, Mar - y,

why you want ___ to do me ___ this way?

Coda 1
Violin Solo

Bridge

I re - mem - ber our first kiss

on the Fourth of ___ Ju - ly. ___

I'll nev - er miss an - oth - er one of those. ___ I'll be

(cont. in notation)

by your ___ side.

Interlude

Gtr. 1

DIFFERENT KIND OF FINE

Words and Music by
Zac Brown, Wyatt Durrette
and Geoffrey Stokes Nielson

cool drink of wa - ter when the sum - mer's mean, _ poured in - to ___ those ___ Le - vi jeans. _ She's

D.S. al Coda

coun - try as the ___ day _____ is long. ___ She make a train take a

⊕ **Coda**

Gtr. 1: w/ Rhy. Fig. 1 (2 times)

Verse

Gtr. 1

2. Tan and lean ___ like a long - neck bot - tle in the pas - sen - ger seat, _ got her hand on the throt - tle. She'll

___ get you there right on time. _____ Lord,

36

Breakdown-Chorus

HIGHWAY 20 RIDE

Words and Music by
Zac Brown and Wyatt Durrette

*Tune down 1/2 step, capo IV:
(low to high) E♭-A♭-D♭-G♭-B♭-E♭

Intro

Moderately slow, in 2 ♩ = 80

*Equivalent to standard tuning, capo III.

**All music sounds a minor 3rd higher than indicated due to capo and tuning. Capoed fret is "0" in tab.

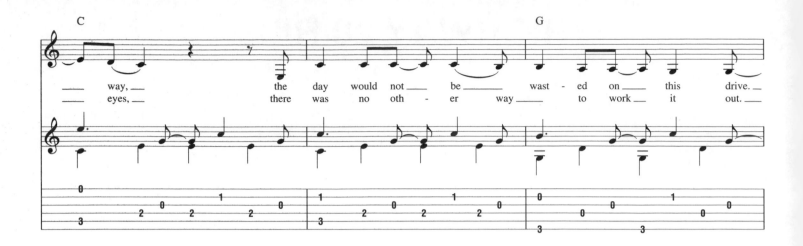

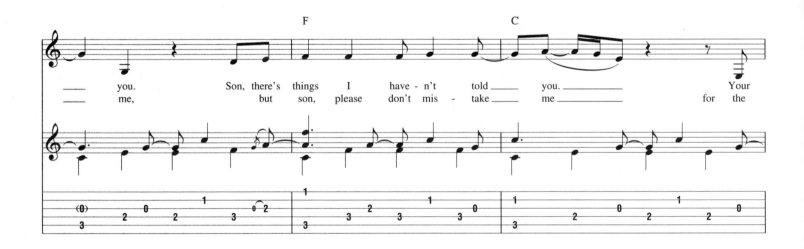

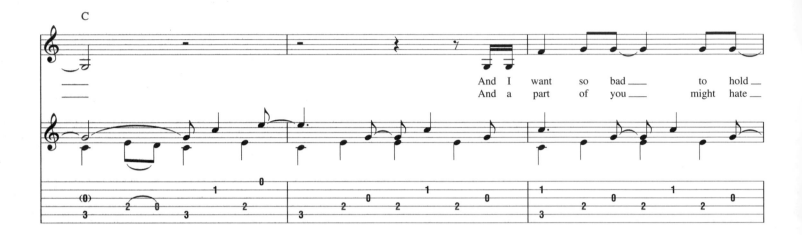

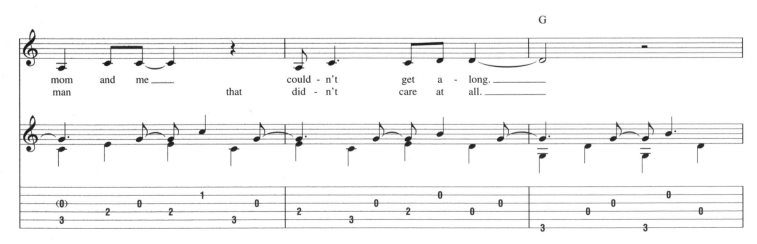

Chorus

So I }
And I } drive _____ and I

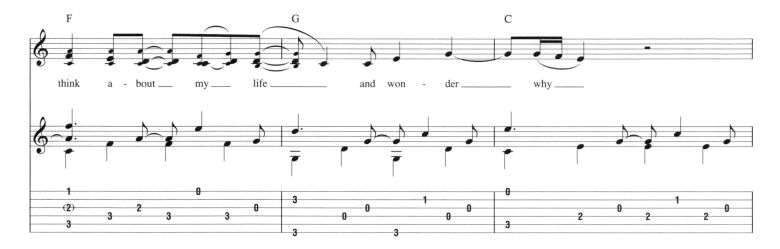

think a - bout __ my __ life _____ and won - der _____ why _____

that I slow - ly die __ in - side _____ ev - 'ry

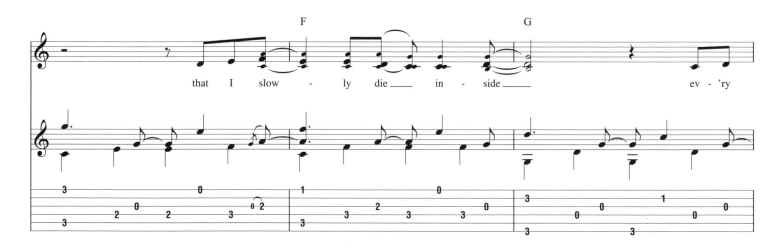

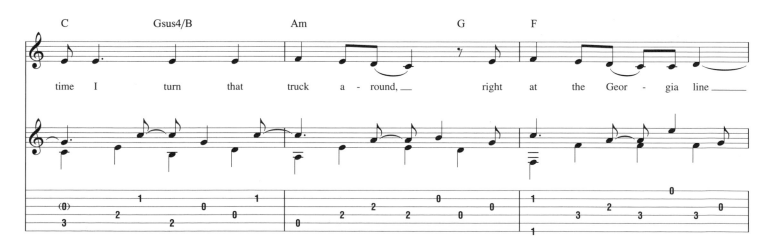

time I turn that truck a - round, __ right at the Geor - gia line _____

Interlude

(Sing 1st time only)

Breakdown-Chorus

So, when you   drive _____   and the   years _____

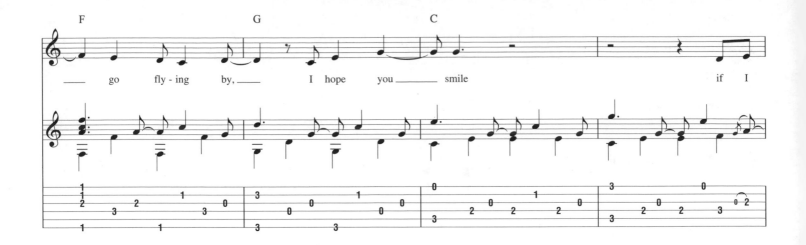

go fly - ing by, ___ I hope you ___ smile   if I

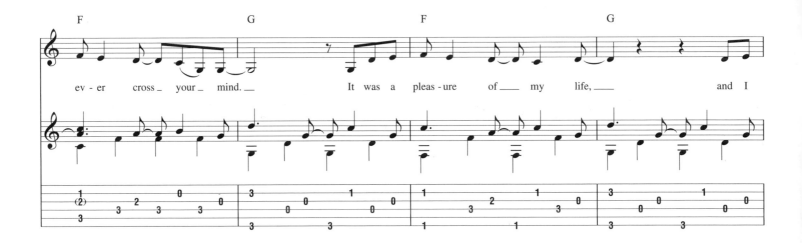

ev - er cross ___ your ___ mind. ___   It was a pleas - ure of ___ my life, ___   and I

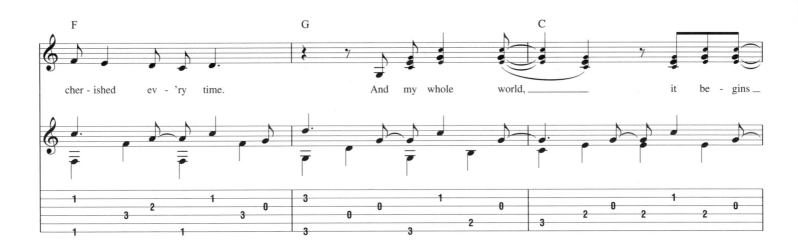

cher - ished ev - 'ry time.   And my whole world, ___   it be - gins ___

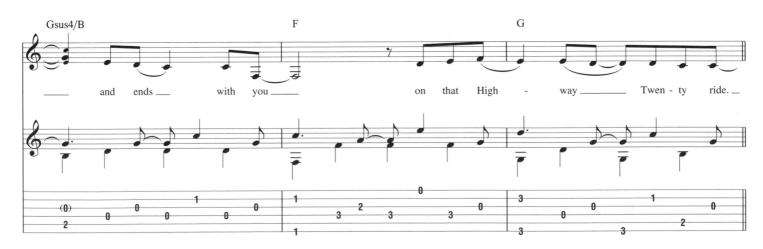

___ and ends ___ with you ___   on that High - way ___ Twen - ty ride. ___

44

IT'S NOT OK

Words and Music by
John Driskell Hopkins

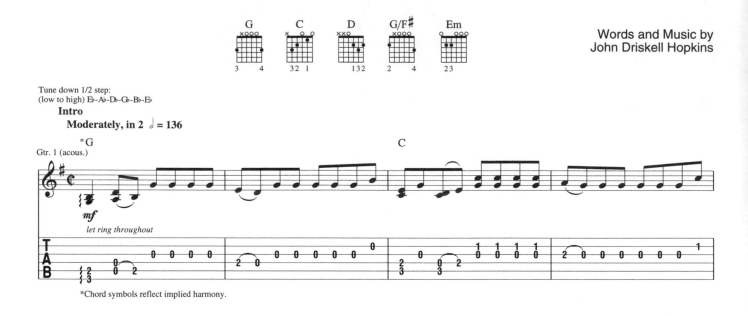

Tune down 1/2 step:
(low to high) E♭-A♭-D♭-G♭-B♭-E♭

Intro

Moderately, in 2 ♩ = 136

Gtr. 1 (acous.)

let ring throughout

*Chord symbols reflect implied harmony.

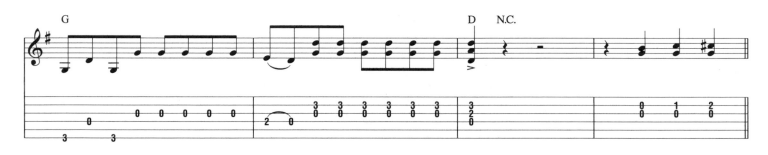

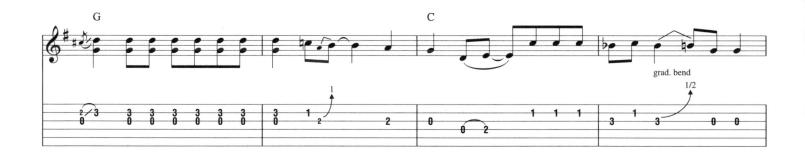

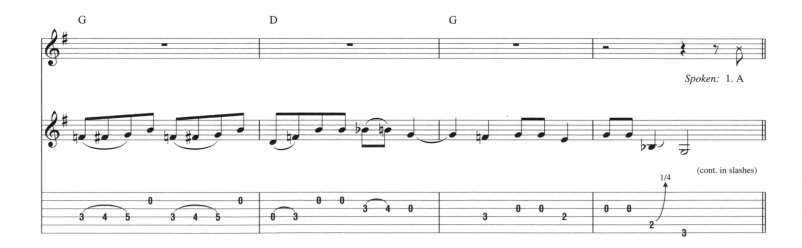

Spoken: 1. A

(cont. in slashes)

Guitar Solo

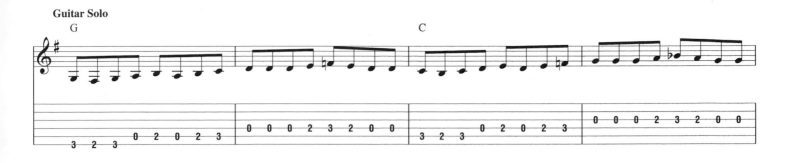

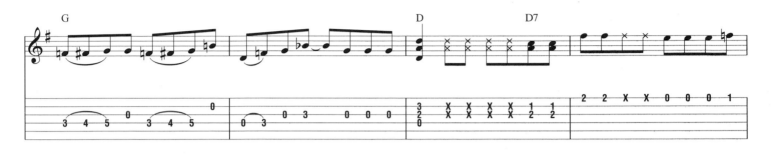

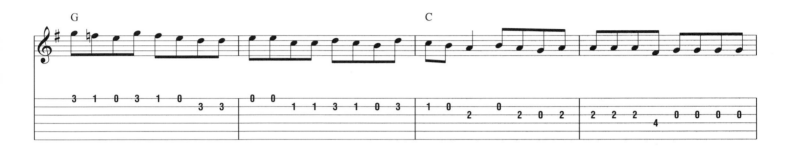

D.S.S al Coda 2

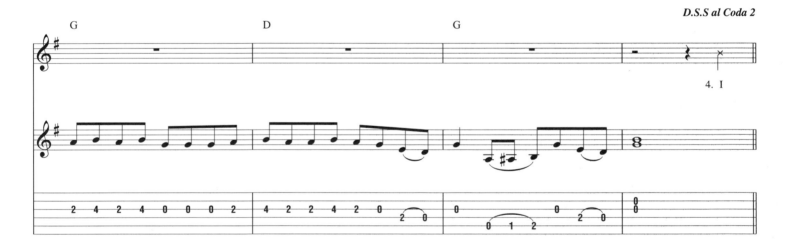

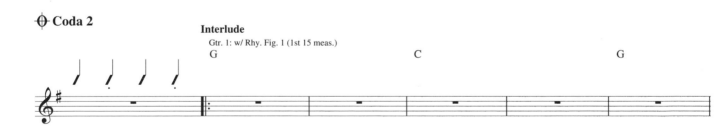

Guitar Solo

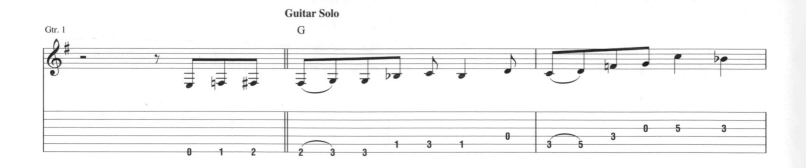

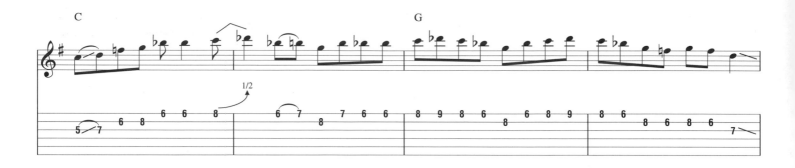

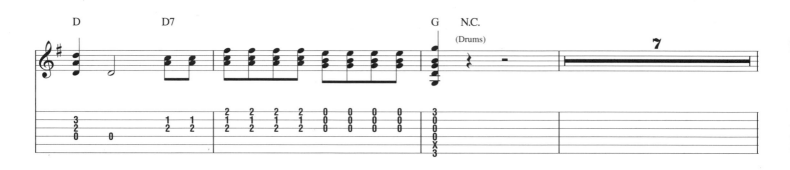

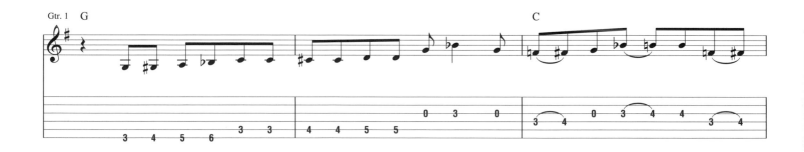

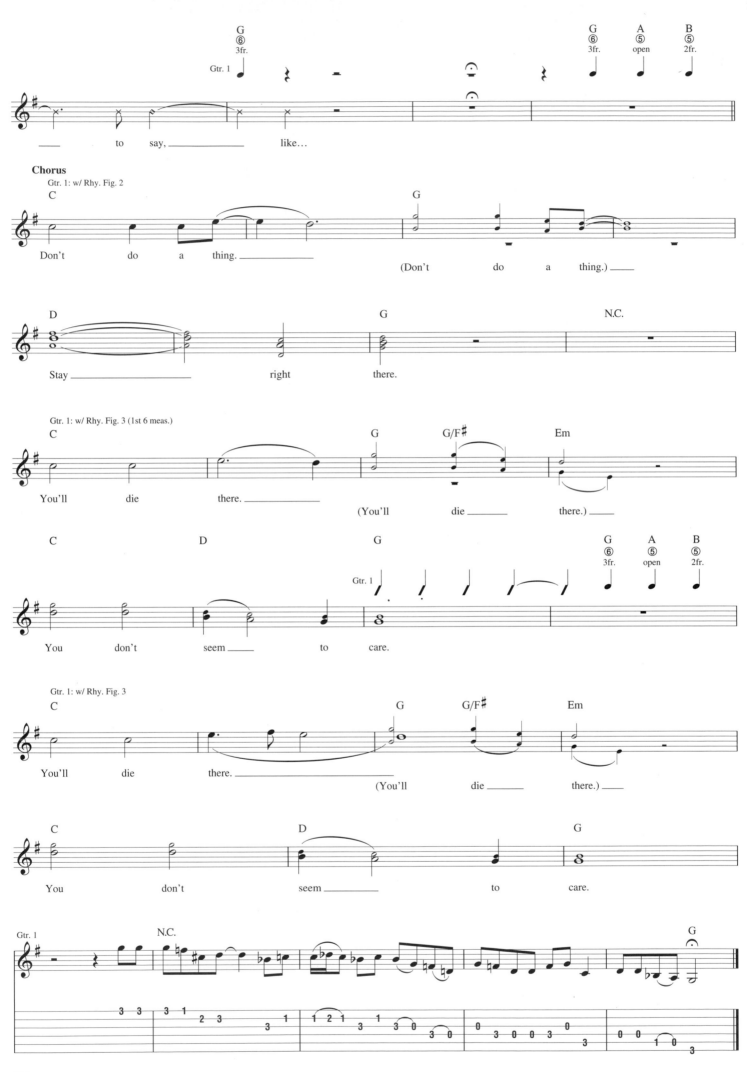

Chorus

Don't do a thing. (Don't do a thing.)

Stay right there.

You'll die there. (You'll die there.)

You don't seem to care.

You'll die there. (You'll die there.)

You don't seem to care.

JOLENE

Words and Music by
Ray LaMontagne

*Chord symbols reflect basic harmony.

held you in my arms one time. I lost you just the same.

Rhy. Fill 1

Gtr. 1

End Rhy. Fill 1

*T (cont. in slashes)

*T = Thumb
on 6th string

§ Chorus

Em   D   C

Jo - lene,   well, I ain't a - bout   to   go

G   C

straight.   It's   too   late,   and I found

G   C   G   D

—— my - self face down in the ditch,   booze — in my hair,   blood on my lips,   a

Em   C   G   D/F#

pic - ture of you — hold - ing a pic - ture of me — in the pock - et of my — blue jeans.

54

Still don't know ____ what love ____ means.

Still don't know ____ what love ____ means. ____

Jo - lene. ____ La la la ____

____ la la la la. ____ Jo - lene. ____ La la la ____

To Coda ⊕

Violin Solo

Gtr. 1: w/ Rhy. Fig. 1 (2 times)

(2nd time, cont. in notation)

____ la la la la ____ la la la. ____

(Sing 1st time only)

Verse

Gtr. 1: w/ Rhy. Fig. 1 (1 1/2 times)

2. It's been ____ so long ____ since I've ____ seen your face ____

or felt a part of this hu-man race. Been liv-ing out of this here ___ suit-case ___ for

way too ___ long. ___ A man ___ needs some-thing he ___ can hold on ___ to; ___

nine - pound ___ ham-mer or a wom-an like ___ you. Ei - ther one of them ___ things ___ will ___ do.

Coda

D.S. al Coda

Co - caine flame in my blood - stream. ___ Sold my coat when I hit ___ Spo-kane.

SIC 'EM ON A CHICKEN

Words and Music by
Zac Brown and John Driskell Hopkins

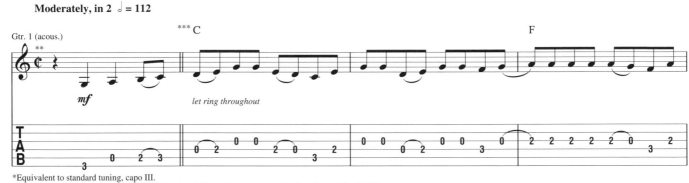

*Tune down 1/2 step, capo IV:
(low to high) E♭-A♭-D♭-G♭-B♭-E♭

Intro
Moderately, in 2 ♩ = 112

Gtr. 1 (acous.)

mf

let ring throughout

*Equivalent to standard tuning, capo III.
**All music sounds a minor 3rd higher than indicated due to capo and tuning. Capoed fret is "0" in tab.
***Chord symbols reflect implied harmony.

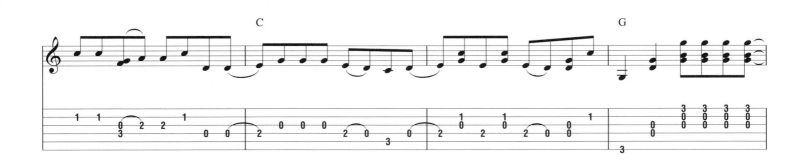

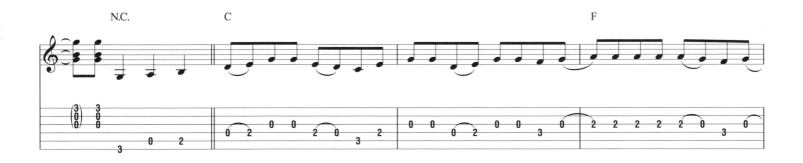

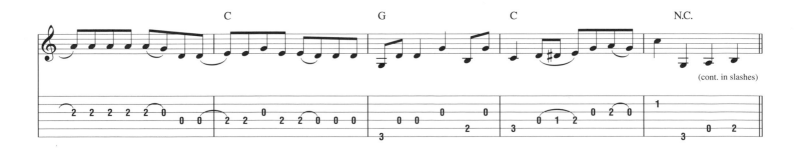

(cont. in slashes)

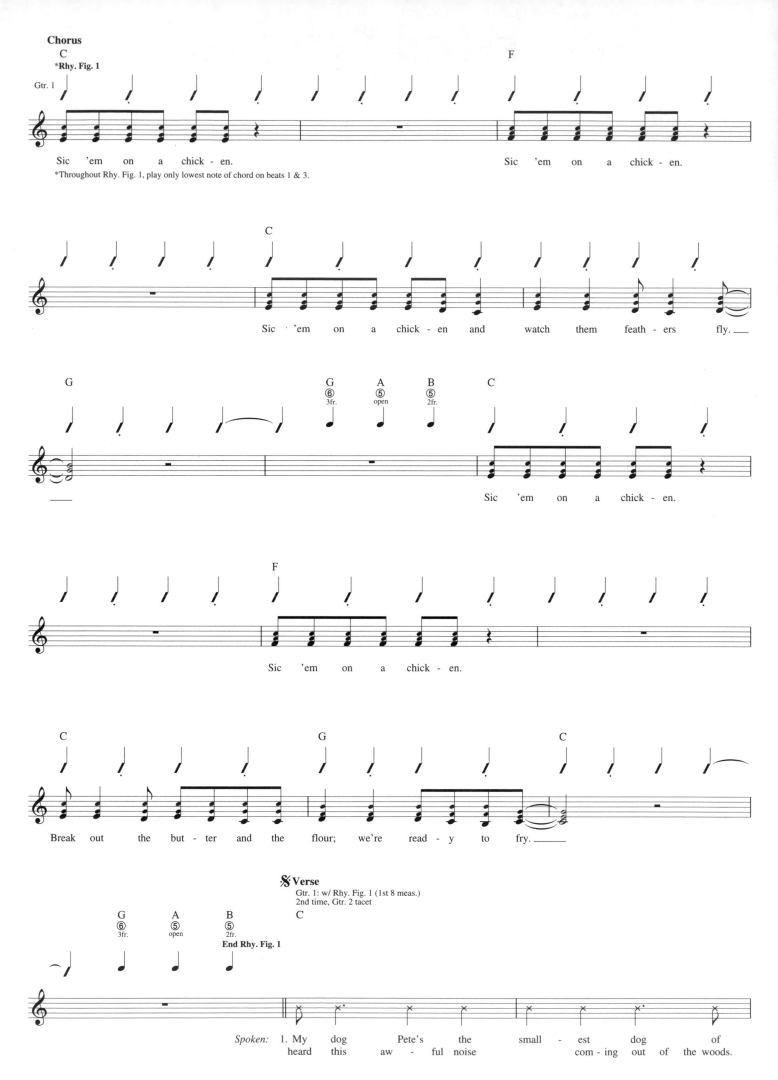

Guitar Solo

Gtr. 1: w/ Rhy. Fig. 1

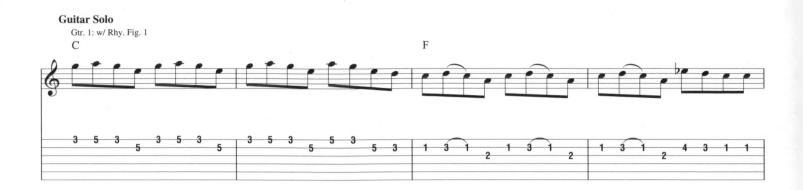

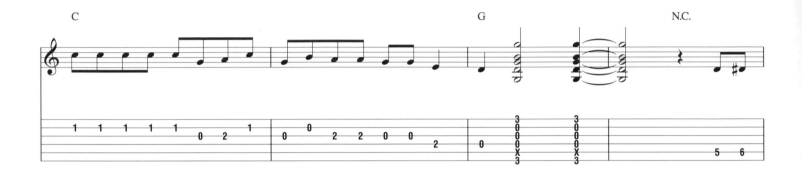

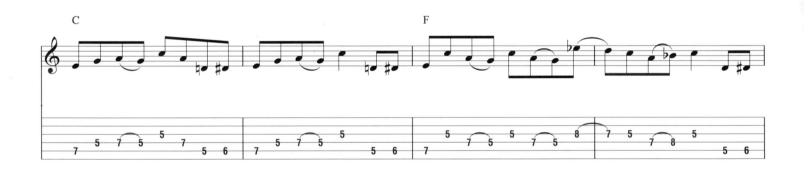

D.S. al Coda 1

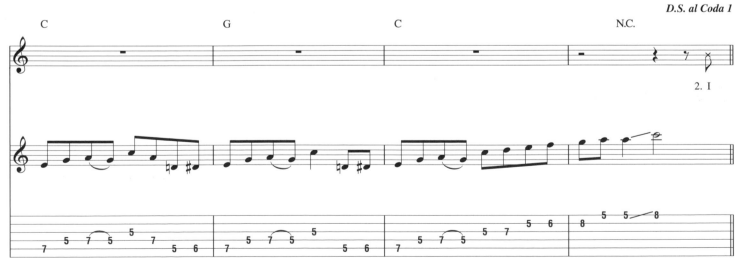

you can get an-oth-er one   for a   dol-lar sev-en-ty-nine.

Violin Solo

Verse

Spoken: 3. O - ver a

cou-ple of years ___ his spurs had grown, and he was-n't safe to keep ___ a - round the home, and he al-most took an eye - ball from Lon-ny's son. ___

And I was in the kitch-en mak-ing fig pre - serves, ___ and I heard that young-'un get kicked in the face, and I

D.S.S. al Coda 2

knew it was the day that that roost-er's gon-na get what he de - serves. So

⊕ Coda 2

Moderately slow, in 2 ♩ = 72

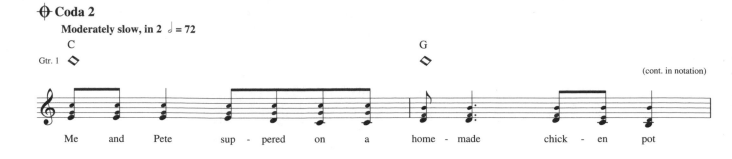

Me and Pete sup - pered on a home - made chick - en pot

(cont. in notation)

Fast ♩ = 172

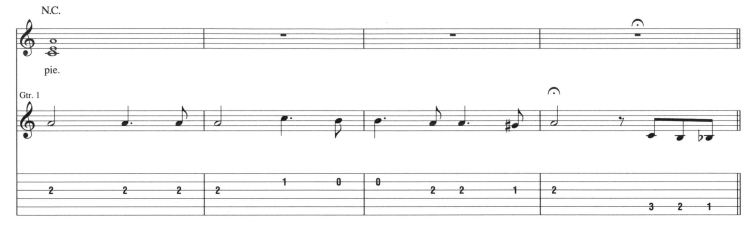

pie.

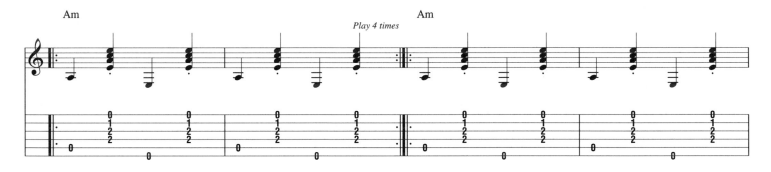

Play 4 times

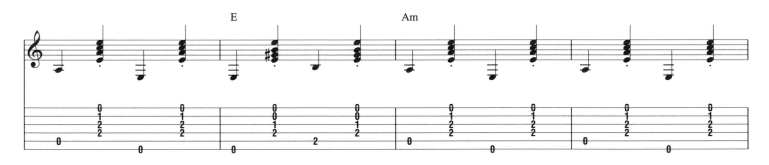

Hey!

GUITAR NOTATION LEGEND

Guitar music can be notated three different ways: on a *musical staff*, in *tablature*, and in *rhythm slashes*.

RHYTHM SLASHES are written above the staff. Strum chords in the rhythm indicated. Use the chord diagrams found at the top of the first page of the transcription for the appropriate chord voicings. Round noteheads indicate single notes.

THE MUSICAL STAFF shows pitches and rhythms and is divided by bar lines into measures. Pitches are named after the first seven letters of the alphabet.

TABLATURE graphically represents the guitar fingerboard. Each horizontal line represents a string, and each number represents a fret.

Notes:

Strings:
high
low

4th string, 2nd fret   1st & 2nd strings open,   open D chord
played together

HALF-STEP BEND: Strike the note and bend up 1/2 step.

WHOLE-STEP BEND: Strike the note and bend up one step.

GRACE NOTE BEND: Strike the note and immediately bend up as indicated.

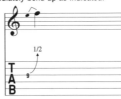

SLIGHT (MICROTONE) BEND: Strike the note and bend up 1/4 step.

BEND AND RELEASE: Strike the note and bend up as indicated, then release back to the original note. Only the first note is struck.

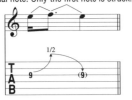

PRE-BEND: Bend the note as indicated, then strike it.

VIBRATO: The string is vibrated by rapidly bending and releasing the note with the fretting hand.

WIDE VIBRATO: The pitch is varied to a greater degree by vibrating with the fretting hand.

HAMMER-ON: Strike the first (lower) note with one finger, then sound the higher note (on the same string) with another finger by fretting it without picking.

PULL-OFF: Place both fingers on the notes to be sounded. Strike the first note and without picking, pull the finger off to sound the second (lower) note.

LEGATO SLIDE: Strike the first note and then slide the same fret-hand finger up or down to the second note. The second note is not struck.

SHIFT SLIDE: Same as legato slide, except the second note is struck.

TRILL: Very rapidly alternate between the notes indicated by continuously hammering on and pulling off.

TAPPING: Hammer ("tap") the fret indicated with the pick-hand index or middle finger and pull off to the note fretted by the fret hand.

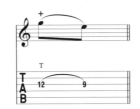

NATURAL HARMONIC: Strike the note while the fret-hand lightly touches the string directly over the fret indicated.

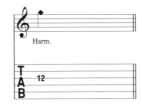

PINCH HARMONIC: The note is fretted normally and a harmonic is produced by adding the edge of the thumb or the tip of the index finger of the pick hand to the normal pick attack.

PICK SCRAPE: The edge of the pick is rubbed down (or up) the string, producing a scratchy sound.

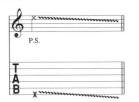

MUFFLED STRINGS: A percussive sound is produced by laying the fret hand across the string(s) without depressing, and striking them with the pick hand.

PALM MUTING: The note is partially muted by the pick hand lightly touching the string(s) just before the bridge.

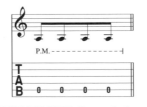

RAKE: Drag the pick across the strings indicated with a single motion.

TREMOLO PICKING: The note is picked as rapidly and continuously as possible.

VIBRATO BAR DIVE AND RETURN: The pitch of the note or chord is dropped a specified number of steps (in rhythm), then returned to the original pitch.

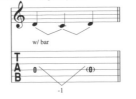

VIBRATO BAR SCOOP: Depress the bar just before striking the note, then quickly release the bar.

VIBRATO BAR DIP: Strike the note and then immediately drop a specified number of steps, then release back to the original pitch.